MW01098782

BREAKER

BREAKER
Sue Sinclair

Brick Books

Library and Archives Canada Cataloguing in Publication

Sinclair, Sue, 1972-
    Breaker / Sue Sinclair.

Poems.
ISBN 978-1-894078-66-5

I. Title.
PS8587.I55278B75 2008   C811'.6   C2008-903160-1

Second Printing – April 2009

We acknowledge the Canada Council for the Arts, the Government
of Canada through the Book Publishing Industry Development
Program (BPIDP), and the Ontario Arts Council for their support
of our publishing program.

The cover photograph was taken by Peter Sinclair.
The author photograph was taken by Cheryl Dipede.

The book is set in Sabon and Buch Condensed.

Design and layout by Alan Siu.

Printed and bound by Sunville Printco Inc.

Brick Books
431 Boler Road, Box 20081
London, Ontario N6K 4G6

www.brickbooks.ca

CONTENTS

Faith

Work

Leisure

Sleep

Faith

Surrender

Sometimes the light, a horse,
gallops into the room
and demands you surrender.
It paws the floor, snorts—
and so you rise out of the low-lying
cloud of the self, the half-dreaming
wakefulness we call love,
and into the cool air of the real.

It shakes its mane impatiently,
rears and kicks, its beautiful body
insisting on what it wants,
pushing its way in. Not
that you're afraid, not exactly.
But it shines straight into your eyes.
And though the heart is small
and cramped, barely large enough for
your own wants, you retreat into a corner,
make do with less. Your only choice
when the world lifts its head
and clarity pours from its back.
Filling the room.

In Spring, When the Earth

Especially in spring, when the earth
is all garbage, and damp smells
of last autumn steam from the ditches.
When even the light is a grime,
thick on the backsides of things—the fire hydrant,
the neighbour's hatchback, the broken
shovel leaning against the wall—
and these things ride their damaged lives
out as far as they can past the washed-up
shores of themselves.

Stepping onto the gravel-strewn porch,
lifting your shoulders back in their sockets,
you wonder what it is you see in this muck,
ants crawling over the doorsill and an infestation
of leaves mouldering on the lawn. Yet even now
your eyes reveal their lustre. As you stare
at the rusted eavestrough, the shadows
arrange and rearrange themselves as always—
you stand in a field of compressed activity,
feel the momentary triumph of the present.
The ants and leaves and even the rot
of last year's ants and leaves grow a halo
when you imagine leaving them. The obstacles
to happiness, the things that weigh on us and demand
we lose a little of ourselves to them, are placed just so,
just in our way, so their hold might be greater.

Wonder

Your mind has emerged
from the night's cold furnace
bright and shining, the dross
washed away. A blue sky has risen
in place of the welter of stars.

As sleep's paralysis slowly fades,
the soul looks around, hoping
for a glimpse of its origin. Tick tock.

The new day hangs from the teeth of yesterday,
which still roams like a lion, prowling through
furniture enshrined in shadow. You have woken up
inside the world's subconscious glittering mind,
have caught it dreaming as it will go on dreaming all day
under the surface of what you know—a banked fire,
invisible, odourless.

Claimed

You know it's no use being attached to things, but
even when the worst has happened, is happening,
the little animal of the heart keeps digging
further into the earth.

You don't want to give up even heartbreak,
even death, the peace that comes in deep pain
when you have no way out.

The insects, the summer heat, declare themselves through you;
you are claimed
and so commit yourself to the blood of this place:
        a rhythmic stillness, a buzzing,
everything in the world
brimming with loneliness
and the sunlit presence of its demise.

We Hope It Will Be Quick

We hope it will be quick, painless,
will happen in our sleep. And that if our minds
give way, there will remain an "I" whose collapse
completes an arc, effortlessly.

So many short straws, and so much conspiring
to lengthen the ones drawn. We hope for strength,
something to help us go on then to give up
even that crutch. However sputtering,
leaky, convulsive, we want to dwell in the world
without condition, even as it ends. We practise
deep in our bodies a fierce acceptance that may be impossible
to achieve, especially now that summer has come,
the day silting into us, heavy fragrance of clover
manuring the lungs.

Sometimes the world seems better for its shortcomings,
what it can't become. The clover expands
like an ocean across the field, sends itself out and out,
never coming back.

Pawel Laughing on the Beach
after a photograph by Nan Goldin

Pawel has just come out of the freezing winter sea, has put on his pants and stands, chest bare, in a warm reddish light. His arms are crossed protectively over his chest, but his head's thrown back, like a madman, laughing—the devil in him tempting fate.

Oh, his radiant skin, the ripple of bones, his chest and arms, his sweet neck! Oh, the soft hairs clustered at his navel. He's doing a favour for his friend Nan, who's always taking these pictures, and because of her and because of the salt and the sun, he's feeling so good he doesn't care that the world will eventually pound him to dust and that it's battering him even now. The sun's delicious and he doesn't give a damn about anything else—so birth and death shrug their shoulders and relinquish their hold on him.

This life and the one afterward want each other, they do. We can feel them trembling (as Pawel is trembling after the cold, cold sea), feel the tug as they strain to come together and are forced apart. It's impossible, except in instants like this, Pawel's arms crossed in memory of suffering while he laughs in delight, his body turned daringly to the camera, dead on—for he has opened his heart to the blood of its next existence even as it pumps in his chest. Somehow he has stepped into another life, straddles them both. And he's aglee, getting away with this for even a split second. After all, he didn't seek it out, can't be blamed for this glitch in the mechanics. And the lens will be refocused in the next second anyway, as it must be, for if it went on—well, it can't go on, it just can't.

Days without End

Spring rages
like a fire in the house,
wants to eat
every splinter.

It forces its way
into buds that explode
like pockets of gas.
Tears new life from the thin
tissue of what was.
The ground shivers.
The trees ache
under the pressure,
look to the sky
for a cool blue rain,

a sign that God
doesn't sit idly by
while creation burns,

that He too endures
the heat of His love,
the great fire
He's pushed upon
the living.

Vanity

So beautiful it can afford to be careless,
the tree has dropped handfuls of white petals
and now leans down to admire itself
in the fragrant pool.

Take even a single flower, see how it mirrors
itself and how pleasing you find
the symmetry. Like you, it wants the world
to be endless—headless and tailless. It wants to be repeated,
again and *again*, for despite its lustre and ghostly appeal,
despite the way its radiance is dispersed across
the field of light, it too is a stranger.
So badly does it want to regain the intimacy
before it knew to cry *again* that it tries
to drown out the rest of the world,
multiplying itself in the eye until nothing else
can enter. And you don't try to stop it.
If anything, you open your eyes wider,
for the impact is gentle compared
to the loneliness that grips you when you
look around and see the green, filtered light,
the matter-of-fact gravel, the slow but steady
differentiation of leaves,

thoughtful and private. Each thing so separate,
so painfully distant, that you begin to pin your hopes
on the impossible, praying that the flower-image
will find a way through, will destroy the masonry
and emerge from the cloud of plaster into another realm.
And you might follow, give up the apparatus of the mind

and step into a place where telling the difference between
this and that means nothing. You'd give almost anything
if you could find a place like that, if anyone could,
if such a place could be said to exist. A place
where the tree and all its flowers are indistinguishable
from the earth itself. Where time falters. Where the eye
blinks and is done.

Awe

Only in this life does beauty
pursue us, pounce on us
with its gleaming eyes. We tremble
as it overtakes us, pulls a like beauty
from our hearts
       and licks us clean.

Only in this life can something
be caught, then released,
and caught again:
           these are savage times:

light flickers across bare fields
and small animals keep their eyes down,
afraid of the lovely shadow
that swoops down from the sky.

Clearing

Wanting the world to prove itself,
looking for wounds, holes in which to plunge
our hands up to the wrists
so as to declare what's real and what isn't,
to shout to the mind's clamouring suitors
that we know, now,
which of them is telling the truth.

Walking above the cliff, through the woods,
wondering what's really there,
what this gives way to—
what, if anything, stands behind the fusty
smell of the firs, the spiderwebs
draped branch to branch. The threads glint,
hint at disappearance, a vanishing
going on before our very eyes:
we come to a clearing where dregs of light simmer—
we come to a clearing—
we come—
we—
(And an echo: do you hear it? Can you
believe in it?)

It's the dark tunnel we want to feel
in things, the bright door in the distance.
And we want to be forced in.
We hope for something that grabs our hands

and plunges them into that yielding place
that some call the beginning, others the end.
Nor do we want to be released
until we admit that what we saw was more
than a mirage. Nothing in the world
is convincing enough. Look down the cliff
to the green-blue swirl,
the ocean's rumbling stomach:
it seems too vivid, somehow,
too solid to be true.

Pelican, Point Lobos
after Edward Weston's photograph of the same name, 1942

The slumped neck, slack-skinned gullet,
the prehistoric, leathery eyelid
fallen forward like a man leaning over
a table, exhausted. A wing half unfolded,
the head limp as though a string has snapped.

You half expect it to stir now that you're here,
but the body is already withdrawing from its old habits,
wet feathers plastered to the throat.
It shames you, who want to own the creaturely
beauty but not the death, not the body
oozed like oil onto the beach. Desire,
not for the first time, seems like a snake
biting its own tail—bent on itself.

You feel overhead the sky's abandoned
consciousness, the blue of its withdrawn eye.
There should be peace in this.
For when the will is gone, what's left
but grace, the mere force of being?
The sand grinds underfoot as you turn to go,
fearing the separation of body and soul
but unable to explain, even to yourself,
why it should be so.

St Phillip's, Rain

An ascetic rain, rail-thin,
beyond being this or that but still falling,
not situated, not placed, unobliged.
Yet its very lack seems purposeful, designed
to reveal something—

as though all that's born arrives
with a wax-like coating, a shell of divinity
that gradually wears off, and this rain
is part of that slow coming-away,
dulling the finish and making the firs seem sunk
deeper in the mire of their mortality. Always
the desire to do more than merely exist,
this plain, forgetting rain
being the only thing we know that doesn't
want to go anywhere but straight down
into the slow-moving world,
the rest of us sick with longing for a god
we no longer believe in, our faces
like spoons, plain and hungry.

Ground Zero

This is the side of things the world has kept from us.

There are reasons, there are always reasons.

Clouds pass through the sky, shy as deer.

The gods mutter among themselves.

A place collapsed.

When one day falters, we look to the next.

But sometimes the days, like everything else, run out.

Forced back into abandoned, half-used moments. Days we
    thought never to have to see again dragged into the light.

We walk carefully, for now we see where more damage is
    possible, the life we've been given already half in shadow.

We stand on one side of our hearts and look to the other.

Wheel Turning

The sun is lowered
like a miner in a cage. Solemnly
it sinks under the horizon,
solemnly night appears.
You concentrate on the slow descent
as though your thoughts could keep
the cable from breaking.

Flowers bend and close
in prayer while others
open, also praying.
The world is on its knees.

Who or whatever can hear, save us,
unless you too have been left
broken-hearted by a machinery
you didn't consent to:

the sun groans,
levered inch by inch
into the ground,
not even a pause before it sinks,
committed to an old promise
that has never yet been broken.

Lil Laughing

after a portrait of Nan Goldin's mother

Lil, darling Lil, who can resist her? Almost eighty and telling you it's not over till the fat lady sings, maybe not even then. Not that she has much time for fat ladies; she loves fitting into her narrow tweed skirt, the seams hugging her slim hips, loves being told she looks younger than her age and knowing it's true. She still loves to dance and flirts with anyone who flatters her. But that's her point: there's no such thing as an age at which you stop caring, she says, sitting on the well-made bed, back very straight, the ring of a long marriage on her left hand. Prim as a daisy, but look at her face! Scrunched up! Gleeful! Like she's trounced you at rummy again.

A bumper-to-bumper smile, but the way her face is tilted slightly upward, with that open-mouthed laughter, she looks a little serious about whatever it is she sees up there. She's clutching at something invisible, and now I think I understand— it's as though an angel has drifted by (for she certainly believes in such things), and she's holding tight to the hem of his skirt, eyes closed, unwilling to let him drift back into the ether. She's a child begging her mother not to go out tonight and, knowing she must, making a game of it. But is she teasing him or in deadly earnest? Is he pulling gently at his skirts, trying to ease them out of her grip? Or does she not see him at all but holds onto the nothing where she hopes such a creature may be?

Anything's possible. If the angel isn't there, and she's trying by sheer force of will to conjure him, she just might do it. And if he *is* there, and if God is merciful, they'll go on wrestling until long after the rest of us have looked away, bored. They'll struggle until they're both exhausted, until they fall down side by side on the bed and the angel forgets who he is and the room forgets how they tussled and she forgets that she wanted anything from him at all.

Drought

And overhead, the birds:
chips of bone in the sky, remnants,
fact of the world's brokenness.

You look up, asking to be forgiven for a crime
you're still trying to locate. You know it's out there,
stare toward the edge of the marsh, the welt of bright water
shrinking before your eyes. A sky of pre-worldly clarity
only confirms your guilt, an inherent misalignment
that keeps you from knowing even a fraction
of what you see.

You cross the heat-ridden ground, the sweet, brittle scent
of sage rising underfoot. So easy to pretend a single word
will occur to you, and that it will do all the good
anyone could hope. The earth is parched and lonely,
relies on dignity to protect it. Each thing hanging
by the thread of itself. Bleating crickets. Rustle of dry stalks.
The silence pushes you toward yourself:
it's time to walk deep into the heart of what troubles you.

Work

Passion

The shimmering, flickering self,
stubbornly risen. Almost chemical, how it ignites
at the smallest gust of wind
and keeps igniting, grabbing the spark
from the given.

Your life builds heat, becomes a furnace
into which pain, love and loss are sent
and may linger for years, a density behind the eyes.

We do not suffer harm willingly
but slowly see it through. This is to do
more than we can imagine,
burning as the stars burn, spreading light
further than we think possible.

Injured Swan
after D.S.

The cargo of mortality has shifted
within you, sinking, dragging you down.
Being is compressed into its purest
form: your back shines, the feathers laid
like ointment over the wound.

You've settled deep into your body,
your self-possession a kind of injury to us,
a reproach. A boy tries to lift you
as though he expects you'll fly
out of his arms, cured.

The Animal Services van rumbles up
and a man with a badge opens the back doors,
reveals the dim interior. We look to you,
falter. The part of us that is swan trembles
before a panic so well-kept. Your pain
is stashed in a vault somewhere inside you,
a document no one dares claim.
It's protected by a combination so
complicated, a string of numbers so long,
it can't be cracked—
yet as the van doors close, we feel like thieves
who've taken something they can't give back.

Fish

His body flings itself into the air
then slaps back down,
a great guffaw. The walloping
seems to have exhausted the whole pond,
which retreats into a deeper solitude.
Insects hum nervously.

It's midsummer, and there is no rest.
The fish concentrates, the willows concentrate,
the old abandoned tire concentrates. It's a risk:
the balance tips as the sun's great incinerator
burns up past lives, claims all our possibilities.
And because some part of us wants to follow it,
the other part resists: the sap rises, blood surges,
keeps us hard at it, pushing our way out
as though the struggle to be born had not ended.

There's an urgency in the slow-paced afternoon:
the fish jumps and snaps at flies not just because he's hungry
but because he's a fish, and this is his attempt
to assert what he is, to do what he must do
if he isn't to be undone. He feels the force of heaven,
the blurred horizon looming in the distance.
He feels the danger. And in the murky water
he's pooling, readying to jump again.

Fruit Trees

Inside all flowering things, the iron purpose
of survival. A lightning rod
conducting need into the heart, grounding
stray impulses. Pollen swarms while the afternoon opens itself.
Petal after petal, darkness sheds its skins.
The sweet genitals of the blossoming world
taken into the mouth.

Nature's opaque gaze returns our own,
the blind staring at the blind. Staticky TV screen
of the apple tree blossoming, a blizzard of interference,
yet the bees board an invisible train and arrive
on time at the platform where the flowers wait.
We take it easy, at rest in the purpose that moves us,
glide into the stupour of noon.

Devotion
for W.R.

Long days spent forgiving fathers
for all they didn't know and couldn't protect us from.
As young men, backs slowly bracing to take on
an inherited weakness. *I don't know*, they said, frustrated
because they felt they had disappointed us
so much already, had fallen too quickly,
born on the steep side of a cliff.

The eyes of some were dangerous, power collapsing
and trying to preserve itself. Some wept like statues,
their own childhoods emerging
and staring helplessly at the world.

Now we just want another chance,
want to retrieve the something beautiful we sank
in them years ago, then set them free
like a net of fish, skins shining. Nothing we learn
can quite cure us of our desire to go there:
to the sandy bottom, where lucent shadows play
and a rusted lure still gleams.

Big East Lake

This is the world, impenetrable, the flat
black pupil that doesn't look at you.
You want to be wooed, to praise it,
instead, you're bored: beauty, what of it?

You feel yourself at the bottom of a well;
love of the landscape can't be roused.
Nature has shifted into your blind spot,
no longer a vision, no longer your ego
revealed to itself. The trees immersed
in growth, occupied by their own being.
The water slips off your paddle.
The shore slips into the water's darkness.

You shift uncomfortably in the bow,
haven't the heart for this.
The light travels a little slower here.
The trees quieter, sober.
If it weren't too late, you'd go back
on whatever promise brought you here.

Control

The city: we are its muscle memory,
its reflex, instinct, its trapped animal self.
We are the leg it would gnaw off to escape.
The ambulance siren wails, open-mouthed,
helpless. Calling us.

We're formed by split-second decisions—this or that—
and have the rest of our lives to wonder about them.
Meanwhile, in every neighbourhood,
behind every door, the silent hum of survival:
fridges wait in halos of static, dogs sleep
like bees in the hive. Seldom can we inhabit
the mystery we are, our houses shut against doubt.
We breathe in, try to reassure ourselves,
tighten our belts another notch.

Winter Morning

The mind's grate, cold to the touch.
Last night's dreams a white ash,
the fire vanished.

A storm of emptiness has blown through,
the light falling from so far away it's a kind
of delay, forestalling absence, darkness...

Two strangers brush their coats off
in a lobby, their bodies turned to one another
like mirrors, reflecting their unknown selves.

As the elevator glides down its shaft,
they brace themselves:
when it opens, all will be revealed,
the contents of their black briefcases,
the secret of their birth.
They always wondered what they carried
that was so heavy.

A block away we stand on the corner,
waiting for the bus.
Still as deer in the snow.
We lean into the silence.

Breaker

A cold-burning brilliance,
distillery of light, green camouflaged
in the ocean's understorey. Your mind is gathered
like a horse about to take a hurdle, ready to leap.
But fascinated by the rising wall, it stalls,
and time seems to slow
while you consider the monumental
fatigue of this immanent failure.

Beauty like a stain bleeds through
the layers of matter,
                    something, somewhere in pain,
the traces of it seeping into this world.
You stand back and watch as the inevitable
takes over: the green recess
of the wave collapses, the light buckles,
the depths recover what was owed.
How helpless you are yet
on the brink of being able to do more,
as though you could punch your hand through
the window to rescue whatever it is that,
trapped inside, haunts the corridors.
You haven't, though, quite got what it takes.
The window shatters anyway, but in the spirit
of denial. So it goes, the heartbreak
of merely standing by as what
dwells here does its living and dying
on its own terms.

Garden

As it flowers, the garden
sinks, a ship being pulled slowly
under the earth. The sail rises
as it goes down.

The flower lets us peer through it
into nothing. Sign of its own disappearance,
it draws everything in—
light travels enormous distances to be there,
its brilliance a railing to hold onto in the dark.

The whole garden like an x-ray,
mysteriously tactile. Hints of the density below.
Shadows beckon, but the only way in
we know is through the light. We roam the visible
as the mast creaks underground.

Away

The voices first, echoing
and tinny, as though trapped inside
an old radio. Then two men with tool kits,
Xs of reflective grey tape across their backs.
They walk side by side along the rails,
toward whatever strangeness inhabits the tunnel,
their muffled footsteps giving nothing away.
They are fading out of time as we know it,
walking into the dimness of an ever-delayed present.
From where I stand, looking into darkness,
the tunnel is not just a tunnel, the Xs not just Xs.
They shimmer meaningfully.

Big, well-fed men a few years beyond middle age,
backs evoking old-fashioned bravado,
talking about home with a shrug of the shoulders.
They amble along the tracks, swinging
their flashlights, light zipping across the dank walls.
The zigzagging light is panicked, groping
for the tunnel's low arc. It's the animal in us
seeking the dimensions that comfort
blind consciousness. Something to hold onto.

They're getting smaller, the Xs smaller,
and my fear for them also recedes,
turns into loneliness. I want to call out,
warn them about some fate they seem already
to know and have accepted. No reason to speak of it,

say their backs. And it's ridiculous, but I could cry,
have in fact to prevent myself. Watching them
go as though they're already gone, passengers
washing through the station, the crowd pressing
around me. And suddenly I seem to see everything, everything!
A delusion, of course: just as quickly it all goes black.
The flashlight beams the last thing I see.

Into the Open

The heavy, stagnant night gives way—
frogs stop grunting as the overheated
sky releases a spasm of light.

The surface of the lake
loses dimension, falsely vivid.
We flatten against the walls
of ourselves as though at knife-point,
the body spot-lit, exposed,
faults glaring.
For an instant everything on earth
loses consciousness, goes limp.
In the ruptured darkness
we grasp what we can and look within.
We prepare to resist the divine spark
that attracts the lightning,
draws it down.

As quickly as it traps us we are released,
but whatever it is out there that wants us
has taken shape,
and we're still stricken when darkness returns.
We've seen the world waver,
know it could hand us over, hostages
to blind force. If there's a name for what happened,
we've already forgotten it.
The sky is empty,
the lake's borrowed face:
we could see clear down to the bottom
and still not understand.

Nesting

Swans groom the light,
prune it with a clip
of their wings, drift
through the clustered lilies.
To the left, stuck
in the shallow mud, a tire:
fat bruised lip, thick
black slug curled into itself,
water lisping around it.
The swans brush against the rim,
consider it a moment
then clamber up industriously,
assuming a purpose
in the worn treads, the functional
given up to the mud's stubborn
suck. By next week
the swans have gathered reeds
and dirt, clay and sticks
into an island, the tire buried
so that everything we've made so far
seems only a beginning,
a crude variation of a kind
of manufacture that ebbs and flows,
hums to itself under its breath.
Nesting, at home, the swans preen
with the insouciance of those
who haven't had to ask forgiveness.
They are not withdrawn,
turn the eggs over in the nest.
Are not lonely.

Fourth View of Bell Island, January 2, 2003

A blue glow, the sky's
depths dredged up.

Abandoned mines,
another junkyard of human
pain, loss. Another hole
in the earth's intestines.

The old houses, naked,
gradually reconcile themselves
to what has gone.
Perhaps there can be a slow
recovery of what we owe:

something here is still alive
enough to feel fear,
and braces itself
against its past, clings
to the old familiar pain.
What has been taken
can be taken again,
the wound not yet so deep
that it's been scraped clean.

Delay

Quarter of an hour, half an hour,
still no train. All of us thinking of home and how
we're not there and will or won't be missed,
how the surface of our life goes on elsewhere
even as we stand here, our absence
snail-paced, cumulative.

We settle in, inhabit ourselves uneasily,
make peace with our half-existence.
Then a dog starts to howl, and though no one
so much as flinches, something tightens
over the space between us.
Some abstract noun, larger and more meaningful
than we care to imagine, has pushed
its way in and is growing bigger by the second.

How could anything suffer so long, so hopelessly?
Yet the sound doesn't relent, and the faces
around me won't let it register,
won't so much as blink. I feel the indifference
on my own face and don't know who I am anymore:
I've fled, but how, and to where?

I picture it, despite myself: the platform ahead, the ambulance,
and the altered faces of those who couldn't stop
whoever it was. The howl becomes the sound
of the soul pushed to the edge of itself,
facing up to a world which it still, after all these years,
is not really convinced it must inhabit.

And because the crowd presses in on all sides
and I can't see and so can't even be sure
it's a dog, I'm frightened, thinking the sound could
in a way be me, a voice from the part of me
I've tried not to know.

Metropolis

The city is a piano, its pedals sunk
deep underground. Commuters in the subway
listen to the instrument groan,
feel their own bodies shudder and give.

There is more memory here than we can manage.
We become paper shredders for obsolete decades—
strips of the past float down from tall buildings,
festoon the shoulders of the unemployed.
History might disappear entirely if we work hard enough.

We all want the day to be our own.
Shoulders rub on shoulders. If everything else were silent,
it would sound like rain:
we are divisible by thousands and remain thousands.

Endurance

The city huddles in its lit cave,
glittering. Snow spins under car wheels;
the heart seizes up as cold seeps into the arteries
and your higher feelings slowly give way,
contract. Your mind begins turning
to stone as the old mineral worry creeps in,
fear of decay, the toil toward oblivion.
Too tired to protest, already feeling
the hardening of the sorrows that relieve
the distances between us, you allow it.
Even the beloved is just a face
pressed under ice.

The snow falls and falls. You endure
the slow shift through the equatorial
from love to loss. Even so, you crane
your neck toward the gauzy clouds,
the snowflakes drifting past the street lights
carelessly, as though sightseeing,
all the time in the world. They are marred
only by the imperfection of gravity,
which carries them down to vanish underfoot.
The compromise is struck. The brown slush
in the gutters pains you. The lit sky pains you.
Nothing that does not leave its mark.

In the Long Afternoons

The sky looks down with a missionary gleam.
The apple trees rise into bloom;
zealously, they rush into the breach, urge
themselves to carry on, do more
as the lengthening summer days
catch up with them. They ripen until they can ripen
no more, striving to split themselves off from their shadows.
But the earth tilts on its axis, and,
sick with fruit, the branches soften
under the straightforward, steady pressure of existence.
They droop, and wasps stew in the carrion mush:
always more than we can bear.
Sooner or later even memory is taken, and we're not sure
what remains. All we know is that the day is darker.
And something has had its fill.

Leisure

Joy

Everything leafs out as though in praise.
Beaky water lilies rise from the pond's stirred muck.
The imagination calls to the world, its inflected echo
coming back to us as light rippling on the back of the real.
Who can say what goes on in the darkened room
from which these idle green days emerge; for all we know
being here might be another kind of absence, a hole
through which our lives come pouring as we fade slowly
in another world. But this world is the one we know,
the one we hold onto, filling ourselves with its visible truths.
We work through the hours, always too few,
packing them into our greedy bodies. Yet we fall prey
to the occasional twinge, hear faintly at our backs
a thrumming, like the bowstring of a shot arrow.
And that sound is what clinches it, our love of this place,
its thin blood penetrating to our very quick.

View from the Train

Wheat stalks drowse away the afternoon,
steep in their unshaken, golden selves,
a tableau of contentment. The earth's heavy,
glowing cargo steadied and sleeping
a deep sleep: the shadows have loosened,
drifted away, migrating into the forest to roost.

Inside the bright gloom of the train
a semi-conscious haze: the smudged glass
imposes a drag on light, which slows
to a standstill. You drink in the slumbering
fields, heady, thoughtless, the sway of the train
like your mind, like a dream swimming
through the narrow canals of waking thought.
Relinquishing hold, you drift into
the thick, golden liquidity of the fields,
weighted and at ease.

But even as your mind blurs, the dark line
of your vision enters the fields like a fox.
It parts the grasses, separating this from that,
blade from blade. Stealthily, it sneaks past
the sleeping guard of the mind and goes
about its business: determines which is which,
staking out the distance between the risen stalks.
It seeks to lose itself but instead parts the grasses
from their kind and thrusts them into singularity,
naked and alone. The stillness you felt earlier
was not stillness; the train moves on.
And then? Does the gap seal over
in your absence, a meniscus of light?

The air in the car is sour with the breath
of strangers. You shut your eyes, think about never
opening them again. But spots of colour drift by
even under your lids. The train pushes steadily on,
repeating the same clicks and clacks, chugging along as if
it will never stop, as if it's forgetting how,
as if it couldn't stop even if it tried.

Homecoming

Wasps dart harmlessly in the lone apple tree, the white blossoms
open like eyes, unblinking channels into the mind's blank
spaces. The cat slides through the fence palings,
slides through your ribs then out again, untouched, unchanged.
Each of these long afternoons has taken something from you,
as though a will not your own has moved into your body.
There is still work to do, and you do it slowly, all day,
first this, then that. You work from a desire under your desire,
a second heartbeat pulsing in your chest. The bare persistence
of time passing, summer's enormous bridge stretching into the distance.

And when the sun fades and quiet descends, you're still there,
have outlasted the day's blunt heat. A thin armour of insects glitters
overhead as you linger on the porch, putting off sleep
like another task. The day is long but your mind is longer.
The night is deep but your mind is deeper. Stars creep over the horizon;
a fertile darkness sinks into the ground.

At Grenadier Pond

1

The willow stands stock-still,
its long leaves like knives divorced
from use so they're no longer knives,
just sharp-edged and glinting.
They don't remember what they're for,
a thousand tiny incarnations
of forgetfulness,
multiple and separate.

2

In its array of not-knives, the willow
leans into itself, supporting its purposeless
cavalry. It seems to be arguing a cause
beyond cause, something inherent in the way
time opens and closes its wings
like an insect poised on a blade of grass.

3

The slow yellowing of leaves
proceeds as though it were a muscle
flexing in sleep, meaninglessly.
Not a yea or nay but a silent, emphatic *is*,
like a man who has done the same work
every day of his life, could do it, he thinks,
if he were dead, so that even his dreams
are a ritual of the present.

4

The trees shift, sway like pack horses,
the weight of non-being equal
to the muscular thrust of all that pushes
into the light, each opened eye. Of the mistaken
belief that life can be made to sit quietly
in the palm of the hand and not tremble,
not much is said.

Exposed

You almost tripped over them: blunt scissors
left to rust in the thick, upholstered lawn.
Heavy, they made you feel the seriousness
of the July heat. Their weight was conducted into you—
six years old and you began to feel your presence as force.
The scissors were both tool and unalloyed consequence.
You dropped them, not quite ready.

Afterward, the quietest afternoons made you nervous,
the rustle of curtains. Summer grinding away.
You turned dead flies over on the windowsill
so their stomachs wouldn't be exposed—biding your time,
waiting to see who'd move first, you or the unknown
person inside you, the untrustworthy being whose small crimes
you wouldn't commit. In the garden you'd realized
what was possible—it struck you like a match.
But you didn't want it to go on burning.

The weight of that strange July afternoon
is still welded into you, added density in the bone.
You don't expect to be freed, but sometimes, in dreams,
the burden transforms itself. The body becomes landscape
and a train flashes through, balanced on the twin rails
of the heart. It disappears into the world beyond,
vanishes in a cloud of dust, and you are empty,
are the middle of nowhere. Alone and suddenly
fearful, you look around for the familiar shadows
that give things shape; there are none. Panicky,
you squint toward the horizon: there, like a mirage,

are the scissors, hanging in the sky. They invite you
to pluck them down, hanging there as if they were destiny,
but you refuse them, have decided your life is not this.
You clasp your hands, squeeze your eyes shut,
hope to wake up before the desire
to reach for them overwhelms you.

Wabakimi Lake

The boulders at rest under water, their hairy pelts,
prehistoric glow,
a deep, unsettling intelligence.

As our paddles skim the lake,
the half-lit bodies loom unexpectedly
from below, the bulk of who we are come to life
and roaming through the sunset gloom
of this submerged landscape.

The forces of mind and heart are everywhere visible
in the sublittoral stillness; you are looking far into the eye
of your intended end, feel the part of you that will return
to earth returning already. The dense lake bottom
draws you and the sun's entrails down, down
into its tawny lair, far out of sight.

Sunburst

Objects in their endless sleep,
hearts beating once, maybe
twice an hour. The clouds drifting
just under the skin of the visible.

And you too are adrift, walking dreamily
by the lake, feeling no burden in you.
But when the clouds part
and the sun forces its way through,
waking life erupts. As the light pours
into the trees, they alchemize—
glory, glory, glory—you've never seen
the leaves so furious, intense, the wood so dark.
A puddle, charged with the sun's image,
lies there helplessly,
a brilliant blind spot, a tear in the foil
that reflects the gods to themselves.

You recover enough to shade your eyes
but your mind circles the edge of this brightness
like a dog circling a slab of meat.
Here's something you want to own and cannot,
something that would burn your fingers,
something that could scorch a hole
right through you, flaming past
without so much as a backward glance.
Faced with this indifference, you feel,
strangely, the rise in the chest that
at times precedes praise.

You cannot conjure up the kind of obedience
that holds the stars in place and keeps the earth
revolving around the sun: what, then,
is this joy? The leaves wave their small flags
as though it were an armistice.
You are free to be a citizen of more than yourself.

Dawn till Dusk

We awaken to find the house
waiting for us,
            patiently grazing
in a field, chewing
the same mouthful of grass
as always.

At the end of the driveway,
a lake of trees,
radiant with stillness.

Things rise up
            in their dignity
and will spend the rest of the day
sinking back
            as our minds start to lag
behind the visible, unable
to keep up with the ever-receding
horizon of what-is.

The world bathes
in the broad pool
of itself,
the day carved
            from the rib of yesterday,
a smooth curve
            like the moon
still poised in the sky.

We rise, the mind dilating
then slowly cinched
as we go about our business, each tending
to what we know
of ourselves,
                    the past
as it lengthens, things taken so much
for granted they seem already
part of that past—

our progress is so slow
as to seem endless, but the blue flame of the sky
begins to fade,
and it happens
            as we knew it must:

the moon's bow slackens;
quietly, deliberately,
time rounds the corner.
                    We ride home
on overheated trains and buses,
and what is in sight
            slowly disappears:
the house wanders off
as night steals into the open mouths
                    of cities and fields.

Outdoor Pool, February

The basin chalk-white as three-o'clock light
surrenders, lets gravity pull it down to slump
against the far wall, the deep end
where autumn's leftover muck ferments.
As the cold settles in, the pool only stares
more deeply from its skinless eye, indifferent
to its fate, passive in the way of someone
taking a pose, someone who plays always
to an audience of ghosts. The swimmers have gone,
but the urge to impress them hasn't disappeared:
something has tampered with the slow surge
toward hibernation, something we feel echoing
in our bones, the question that precipitates
everything we call the self.

The blue sky intensifies.
The unlit lamps mounted on posts look on
with a lost-my-voice helplessness.
The chain-link fence gleams.

Blackout

The city vanishes. The electric hum
sucked away, leaving a vacuum.
It's as though we've woken from a dream
halfway to the ground. We look at our hands,
which we expect will be the first to disappear.
A clattering echo as a raccoon lumbers
away from a row of dented garbage bins,
in its gait a hint of satisfaction
at the erasure foreshadowed here.

We prowl the streets, greet everyone
as the intimate strangers we've become.
Around each voice, a halo of silence
that enlarges in the dark.
You could say history has ended, and now
we wait for a new mythology to emerge:
soon a line of bicycles glides past, following
the glow of a single headlight as though
chasing a butterfly that seems on the point
of vanishing into the past.

Fifth View of Bell Island

Silence erects itself like a building.

At a distance, snow falls
almost not at all.

The Raelians say
they have cloned a child.
The soul becomes lonelier.

Snow thick in the air now.

In the harbour, a seal bobs up—
its dark eyes see
another seal buried deep
inside you.

Quiet

The sky a deadbolt slid firmly
into place. The earth is lonely:
a dog barks its head off, trapped
in the slow afternoon. When he gives up,
the silence is another lock on the door.

The heart pushes on us like a stone
no one can lift. We want so much
from this life but can only glimpse it.
We wander from room to echoing room,
always only the surface of what we seek:
smoke rising through the floorboards, the faint
perfume of the earth burning, deep in the well of itself.
That something we have never seen affects us so completely:
we are the healed skin of its molten core.

Tell It to the Night

I

Nobody loves you
like the one who left you—
the hard truth you're weary of,
wanting to forget, the blues
taking you into the heart of trouble
so deep you can't remember
how you got here. Dancing close,
the body giving up its shame,
swaying in the emptiness that's left
when what could have been drifts away,
your arm draped hopelessly
over someone's back like a sigh,
like the matter in the body sighing,
envious of the spirit, its longevity.

The instruments shine, feel within them
the same loneliness,
attracted by the beautiful sheen
of sweat on your skin. The notes sink
deeper into the night, into your skin,
prodding you gently, recalling you to your sadness,
for it's late now, time to remember all that has
gone wrong, all that has been lost,
all that has left you here,
music's slow liquor passing through you
as all that mattered has
passed through and gone on.

II

After a beer break, the band reappears,
faces gleaming. We're bold and uneasy.
The melody begins, a run of notes—
the trumpet shines. The floor
quivers under our feet like a horse
all muscle, ready to run.

As the bass player picks up the pace,
the old hall quakes. We dance past midnight
under the aegis of the past. Our weight
pushes nails out of the boards:
between sets, a man in a blue suit
taps them back in, careful
as though this were the spine of the living.

III

The night slowly, slowly
dances the blue out of the evening
and into the deeper regions
of the heart, slowly, slowly,
blues-ing you out of the evening
and into the deep regions
where you risk
what you love, always a price,
dancing past midnight,
blues leaching into darkness, becoming
the deeper regions of what you are,
the yearning once midnight's gone
and there's nothing left but the night
dancing slowly, slowly.

Sleep

Evening

Swallows skim the pond, lilting,
tweak insects from the air.
They cross and recross an invisible border,
bodies gleaming with purpose,
violet backs armoured against doubt.
You imagine them tucked under a cliff, sleeping
when the winds blow in from the cold eternal.

With evening, your mind feels a loss
of habitat, disorienting. The blurred, long-distance
sighting of immortality as sleep closes in.
The salt of dreams is deposited behind
your eyes, a glimpse of the distinctions mined
from the visible. Confirmation of your poor,
earthbound status, for what are dreams
but the mind running over and over its lack?
God, if there is a God, doesn't dream.
You wonder if the sparrows do—they must—

for they, like you, inhabit a shadowed world.
Yet they seem to sleep unharmed while you
are up late again, worrying. In the dark unsheltered sky,
even the stars seem to have filtered out doubt:
they shine in the coal black night, raw and enviable,
not fragments but each one the whole you've lost.

Driving North

Moths in the high beams, a nerveless fire
so sudden, so bright, you feel a surge
of power in your brain. It overloads.
The visible panic, frantic wings.
An unseen net pulling them forward
as they struggle to escape.

A shot of adrenalin and the moths
disappear, whisked—fluttering, afire—
into the mind's secret recesses.
Years later they're in your dreams.
Sleep reveals them in their entirety,
the hairy bodies, ragged wings—
potent, stinging glimpses of fates
impossible to contemplate.
Things you get through by refusing
to imagine them. Things you just get through.

Suburbs

Night holds up a mirror on all sides;
there is a depth in things you haven't accounted for.
The bungalows return your gaze; their lost dignity
surfaces and they stare at you, trying
to import meaning into their small lives.

Vinyl-sided, slow-witted,
they insist they didn't mean for this to happen,
this sameness, shackled to their own kind
like cattle transported slowly nowhere
in a broken-down truck. This is what happened to them,
not what they are. And they know the privilege
of even this adequate existence. Ashamed,
they lower their heads as children do
who think they have done something wrong
in being born. You too bow your head,
wish you could divest yourself of scorn.
A woman climbs into a car, will drive until
the motor dissolves her troubles.
Further up the street a man lifts a blind,
looks around, and wonders what it can all be for.
He hopes no one will answer.
He is embarrassed to have to ask.

Waiting

Night lays its weary head
against your roof, settles in.
Roses swell in the dark.

In neighbouring houses, children stare
at televisions like theologians. The stars
no longer visible, no longer means to an end.

Comfort comes slowly
as you climb into bed and sleep loosens
the bandages. In your dreams
you hear the trees rustle and whisper and hiss
their disappointment. For you are not

the serum, not the powerful, Herculean,
mythical, myth-bearing creature they need.
If only you could whisper back,
tell them how much they mean to you.
But it wouldn't matter:
fact is, they're waiting for someone.
And you are not that someone.

Waiting for the Forks

The things that can and do
go wrong: Grandfather's birthday, a family reunion,
and no forks for the cake

because the caterers had a lot on their minds,
what with the champagne and Aunt Julie
in her thigh-high kimono—

in fact no one realized until now, so what can we do
but make airplanes from folded napkins,
nibble the frosting and kick the dog

under the table while they fetch forks
from down the street, which will take awhile
but that's okay because Grandfather

has a lot to remember, enough candles on the cake
to light the darkest corners of his mind; suddenly he can see
all the rooms of his life, and he was planning to make

a speech, has been trying to think of just what to say,
waiting for it to come, but now surprises himself by deciding
he won't speak, won't reveal himself, not to a soul,

and when he's in heaven he won't come back
and tell them what it's like. He's just this minute
decided he'll step through the last door

willingly, and that means no backward glances.
Besides, what if he tries to come back
and can't? What if the threshold vanishes

as soon as he crosses it? And even if he could reappear,
they might not recognize him—though that's
hard to imagine. In any case, his mind is made up,

and he hopes they'll make the best of it.
A camera appears and he poses obligingly
with a pair of grandsons on his lap,

the children's hair wispy and colourless as his,
their eyes fixed on him as his are fixed
on the red-crepe-paper-covered table:

waiting for the forks, waiting for the camera to flash,
he looks at the plate in front of him, the slice of cake
he's about to eat.

Beyond Faith

Night rears over the earth,
its thousand hooves glittering,
its chest rippling, muscular.

Your body fears even its own
breath, afraid of being singled out:
you didn't know the gods
still appeared in the world,
and can only pray for them
to gallop off into the far reaches.

Their immensity is concentrated
in the streak of light that represents the world
to the eye. You suffer their undiluted brilliance.
Power runs loose, is not kept safely
under lock and key in the other realm
as you hoped. You want to turn away,
but the cold, fiery light has nudged you out
to face the beauty of your creaking planet.

The stars gaze down at your weak face
and hands, your soft hungering mouth:
you are sick from yourself, tired of your own image
everywhere you turn. Too late to beg for faith,
you stand paralyzed as the stars open and open,
revealing something that is not belief, not hope;
something harder and more radiant than that.

Closure

Darkness sediments
in the house. Night, a whetstone
on which the blade of the mind
is ground. The dull shine
of your thoughts
swells in the dark.

The crickets, fricative,
a shower of sparks
illuminating the silent
road, interrupted
now and then by a car speeding
wingless down the yellow line,
humming. It recedes,
enters the tunnel
of distance, swallowed
by the depths that rise
from the ground at night.

The stillness strips us bare:
we can hear everything,
the rustle and creak of the house
after the crickets cease.
The moon rises as we twitch
and drop into sleep
like frogs leaping into a pond.

Fairy Tale

The knight didn't kill the dragon, only maimed it;
he plunged his lance into the thick flesh
and fire poured from the wound but the heart kept on
pumping its combustible blood through the canals.
And though the dragon was now slow
and harmless and couldn't terrorize the countryside,
the knight wasn't a hero. The beautiful maiden
turned away when she saw the poor beast
he brought limping into court, harnessed by a thick rope
that was more to guide than tether him.
She hid her face and backed into her private rooms,
her ladies scurrying at her sides.
The trumpets were lowered in shame.

He looked at the dragon, and the dragon
looked back at him, and he knew then that they were
twins, born together into the misfortune of this moment.
The armour and the flesh could not in that instant
be told apart, nor have they been since.
The rope that joined them joins them still as
they wander over the gilt-edged pages of storybooks,
depending for their livelihood on the kindness of strangers
who offer them bowls of thin soup
and a place to sleep for the night.
No one asks them to stay, nor are they asked
to tell their tale, and for this they are grateful:
the injury has gone so deep they don't know
where to find it anymore.

Breakwater

In the 1990s a breakwater was built using erratics that once dotted the shore of Flatrock, Newfoundland. Erratics are blocks of rock dropped by retreating glaciers.

The boulders lifted from the shore,
raised in slings as though being rescued.
Embarrassed, their awkward bodies
dangled in mid-air as though they had been
woken from sleep, taken unprepared.
Piled like rubble in the bay,
they stare out from the breakwater
as if forbidden to speak, using ancient
telepathy to send a warning.

We were afraid of something they
represented, their blank faces
looking somberly into the future,
monuments to a mistake we had yet
to make, traces of something
we wanted to erase before it could exist.
We haven't eluded it. No better off,
we've forfeited consolation, won't know
where to go in our grief.

We've cast ourselves deliberately out
of our own future; it is a locked door
on which we will bang and bang,
looking for answers, looking for silence,
a moment to think through our lives
before they're lost.

Speak, Stone

The burden,
the unconsumable,
not the ashes
but whatever it is that survives
and will not be dispersed.

Cold sinks into the body
and lies still, like an animal
breathing. Thus inhabited,
we yield to stark, unnarrative
matter. Everything lies open,
spread feast-like before us,
inviting, yet can't be touched,
can't be moved ahead.
Like a photograph:

frost-riven cement,
tree limbs thick with snow.
Naked as the dead are naked.
Inside everything, the worn
fragments of self.
They harden and harden:
to live is to carry forward
the weight of dying.

Falling from a Great Height

A hardened, varnished afternoon.
Gulls pick at dumpsters
as boys ferry their basketball back and forth
over the centreline, stewards of the court.
Heat pours off the tarmac; they play deeply,
soulfully, until the day lopes off to the western
horizon and the game loses its appeal.

They go inside as darkness trembles
over the neighbourhood like an alcoholic's hand.
A car passes; the sound of its engine wraps our minds
in its cocoon. We close our eyes, forget at last
what we're made of and sink into the elsewhere
that cast its invisible shadow all day.
Heat drifts from room to room
not wanting to disturb anyone.

The garbage rots leisurely in the dumpster,
its rich odour attracting raccoons. Inside,
children and adults dream of changing places,
long for each other in the dark.

Meteor Shower

The soul stares at the night sky,
its doppelganger. They pretend
they're invisible to each other,
but they watch. Uncertainty divides them.
Suspicions exchanged in silence.

The constellations are trappers' lines.
Meteors limp across the sky,
tails aflame: they have escaped,
but not unscathed.

The fiery ordeal distracts us
from the darkness. The sky reaches deeper
into its pockets, pulls out an empty hand.
Against the firmament, the town clock
seems to have hopelessly old-fashioned ideas
of time. Hours and days give way to wilderness.

Policemen with dogs search for a thief
while the meteors glow and vanish overhead.
The buttons on their suits gleam like eyes
as they scour the riverside, the cold air
drawing their breath away.

Near the river, a stone abutment
from a bridge that burned down years ago:
it watches its own history
repeated in the night sky.

Astronomy

The universe announces itself: a dark hull
draws up on your shore. Glittering and strange,
it puts you in sight of your weakness.
The engine shudders and is still.

The weight of that vessel remains wedged
in your side, inoperable. The night sky becomes
a resting place, its familiar silence
attracting the terminally ill, meaning anyone
who has felt a twinge as the mind
recognized itself in the body.

Astronomers think they can see years pass
in split seconds, but nothing could be slower,
more awkward. There is Carina, bound
by its own brilliance, a listing keel, heavier
on one side than the other, Canopus
a burden of light in the hold.

Telescopes become a medical instrument,
a way for the dying to examine themselves.
You look through them into your
own eye: the universe limps deeper
into your body, tips you to one side
as you lean to the other.

Sixth View of Bell Island

The ferries pass like strangers.
All night heaven and earth
draw closer together,
threatening to collapse
into each other.

Old unforgiving loves hold us
accountable. Their claims ferment
in the blood as we stand here,
waiting for a pathway to open
in our brains, hoping
something will click.

The ferries have memorized
themselves, no longer need the mirror
each offers. They file past
with no sign of recognition.
We feel an irreducible shiver:

failure begins to seem a refuge.
As though once admitted,
it will demand nothing more of us.

Waves place their hands carefully
on the shore, wait for the moon
to tug them away.

Longing

Tired of being alone, especially at night.
The stars broken down in the sky, engines stalled,
shining, waiting for rescue.
The height of things stares down at you.

You settle into the night's own loneliness,
let the universe expand, stretch like a curing hide.
Someday the absence on the other side
will show through, unquantified:
if history is an animal, this is its pain,
an unspoken reproach, the throbbing in the vein
that accompanies the inevitable going forth,
you or someone like you taking the place
of the unborn, feeling their stare.

Is the great beauty of things somehow visible to itself?
If so, is it enough? For how quickly it vanishes,
becomes its own ghost. And then there is you:
you have only the barest idea of what you'll leave behind.
History must feel its failures vividly.
You wonder if it heard the chorus fade away
when you were born, for you grew up
knowing nothing of the echoes that surrounded you,
still less of the voices that will be lost when you leave.

Portugal Cove, Night

The dock lights glow, involuntary,
instinctive. Beyond them, something takes
the form of darkness and enters the world,
a prowling animal laying claim to his territory.
A fire kindles in the gut, a warning—
you're standing so close to this creature
and his infinitude of names.

Shivering, you realize he's the one
you've called on to keep chaos at bay—
how foolish you were. You feel his breath
on your neck, the breath of more
than birth, more than death, beyond
your two great abilities. Different from cold,
harder to resist. He pads deliberately closer,
mouth wide, filled with stars.

This is the form in which he is most terrifying—
his pupil has opened so wide he can see
everything at once, just as it is, the sum of his will.
He will take what he chooses. You look as far
into his eye as you can bear, try to seem unafraid.
The dories lie open on the wharf, white bodies like
split shells. The cliffs darken until they cannot be seen.
This is not the god you dreamed of.

Asleep

A wasp-like hum in the room,
the something-going-on that passes for silence
in these quarters, for we want to believe in silence,
that our repose leaves nothing behind, empties all the chambers,
takes the present into our dreams with us and leaves
a void that works like acid on all that was.
Car headlights on the wall mean nothing,
the cramped, ungrowing furniture, nothing,
the church spires, tired bells, nothing.
They are but the residue of day, less than echoes,
the last creaking stair on the way out of perception.
We have come to an agreement: tired of the world
in its inalienable unlikeness, we will give up coaxing it out.
So the night darkens, the curtain drifts
out the window, the very lateness of the hour ceases.
We sleep side-by-side with eternity, and never touch.

Thanks

Versions of some poems have appeared in the following literary journals: *The Fiddlehead, The Malahat Review, Arc, PRISM international,* and *The New Quarterly.* Poems have also appeared on the websites of *Maisonneuve,* the Canadian Parliamentary Poet, and *Poetry Daily.* Thanks to these publications and organizations.

Thanks also to the OAC for financial support.

Thanks to Jan Zwicky for letting me hear and see these poems through her ears and eyes. I consider myself lucky.

Thanks to Alayna Munce for being first reader of this collection and also my copy editor: it's kind of an embrace, being there at the beginning and at the end.

Thanks also to Shane Rhodes for subsequent comments on the manuscript; thanks to Michael deBeyer and Lauren Corman for comments on individual poems.

Thanks to the good people at Brick—especially Kitty Lewis, Maureen Harris, Alan Siu.

Thanks to my father, Peter Sinclair, for the cover art.

Thanks to my other friends and family.

And thank you, Nick, for your editorial work—and for the pleasures of life in the Ivory Tower.

S ue Sinclair has written three previous books of poetry, *Secrets of Weather & Hope, Mortal Arguments,* and *The Drunken Lovely Bird.* Her work has been nominated for awards including the Gerald Lampert and Pat Lowther Awards and the Atlantic Book Prize for Poetry. *Mortal Arguments* was a Globe 100 title. Sue grew up in Newfoundland and now lives in Toronto, where she is doing graduate work in philosophy.